MW00896395

HEAVEN'S SONS REVEALED ON EARTH

Ian Johnson.

Published by
His Amazing Glory Ministries
4 Ewing Road,
RD4, Tuakau, 2694
New Zealand.

Dedicated to the memory of

Calvin Miller, who passed into glory in 2012;
Pastor, Poet, painter and an amazing writer and
scribe who has inspired me, guided me into
union with Christ through his writing and blessed
me for many years.

CONTENTS:

ONE - Dreams and Visions.

The Church was founded on dreams and visions. They are the natural supernatural part of the Church that is being restored today.

TWO - Working with Angels

Forty eight people are recorded as having had two way conversations with Angels. Angels are mentioned three hundred and seventy five times in the Bible and play a huge part in the plans of the Lord.

THREE - Prophetic Intercession and Motivation

In order to see heaven revealed on earth, Intercessors need to walk like Jesus walked. He only ever did what he heard the Father say or the Holy Spirit do.
Motivation of the heart will play the leading role in apostolic intercession.

FOUR- Kingdom Fathers and Heaven's Sons

Apostolic Fathers are called to be gate openers not gate keepers. Fathers who move at this level inspire sons to follow.

FIVE -Borders and Gates

Gates we open determine the borders we live in. Opening the gates of the Lord brings generational blessings. Opening the wrong gates brings generational misfortune.

SIX- A Kingdom of Intimacy

The true power of an Apostolic Father is intimacy with the Lord; no intimacy, no power. Stepping into the heart of the Lord brings true life.

INTRODUCTION:

Welcome to the Heaven's sons revealed on earth. This book is designed to get you on the road to a supernatural lifestyle that will see the process of transformation from Christian to son of the Kingdom. All Sons and Daughters are called to walk with God and to enjoy the realms of heaven, but most importantly, we are all called to release heaven on earth. This just won't happen while we remain committed to a system that prevents the maturating of sons and daughters. The worlds are groaning for the revelation of the Sons of God and a system that acts as a gate keeper and not as a gate opener for the King won't enable us to see the need to walk where we are all called to walk. The Church is called to be that gate opener, and Fathers and Mothers in the Church are called to show the Sons and Daughters the gates. This book is an invitation to revolution and reformation in the body of Christ. It is not to dismiss the Church, but to lift her up as the true gate opener, so that the King of glory may come in.

DREAMS
AND
VISIONS

DREAMS AND VISIONS

When God speaks He speaks in spiritual language. For instance, when Nicodemus came to Jesus in John chapter 3, his thinking was natural but Jesus was teaching him to think in spiritual terms. The desire of Jesus is still to teach us to think in spiritual language. It's important for us to understand that we need to step into the mind of Christ in order to think like him and to see like him.

One type of spiritual language that I feel is almost totally neglected in church and ministry government is dreams and visions. When we learn a different language like French or Hebrew, we also learn how to think in that language, it's at this stage of learning that the speaking of the language becomes easy. In order to interoperate the languages of the Spirit correctly we need to learn how to think in those languages.

The Bible says that these languages of the spirit are a last day's phenomenon;

Acts 2:17 says, 'In the last days,' God says, 'I will pour out my Spirit upon all people. Your sons and daughters will prophesy. Your young men will see visions, and your old men will dream dreams.

In the Old Testament; Joel 2:28 (NLT) Then, after doing all those things, I will pour out my Spirit upon all people. Your sons and daughters will prophesy. Your old men will dream dreams, and your young men will see visions.

PART ONE – DREAMS.

 Job 33:14-16 (NLT) For God speaks again and again, though people do not recognise it. He speaks in dreams, in visions of the night, when deep sleep falls on people as they lie in their beds. He whispers in their ears.

This scripture tells us that God is constantly speaking in dreams and visions of the night. In this book I want to look at some dreams to help us understand just how significant this language of the spirit really is.

Jacob's Dream
Genesis 28:10-19; (NKJV) Now Jacob went out from Beersheba and went toward Haran. So he came to a certain place and stayed there all night, because the sun had set. And he took one of the stones of that place and put it at his head, and he lay down in that place to sleep. Then he dreamed, and behold, a ladder was set up on the earth, and its top reached to heaven; and there the angels of God were ascending and descending on it. And behold, the Lord stood above it and said: "I am the Lord God of Abraham your father and the God of Isaac; the land on which you lie I will give to you and your descendants. Also your descendants shall be as the dust of the earth; you shall spread abroad to the west and the east, to the north and the south; and in you and in your

seed all the families of the earth shall be blessed. Behold, I am with you and will keep you wherever you go, and will bring you back to this land; for I will not leave you until I have done what I have spoken to you." Then Jacob awoke from his sleep and said, "Surely the Lord is in this place, and I did not know it." And he was afraid and said, "How awesome is this place! This is none other than the house of God, and this is the gate of heaven!" Then Jacob rose early in the morning, and took the stone that he had put at his head, set it up as a pillar, and poured oil on top of it. And he called the name of that place Bethel.

Jacob had an amazing dream in Genesis 28 where the heaven opened and a stairway appeared between heaven and earth. The Lord appeared at the head of the stairs and Angels ascended and descended. The Lord promised the land to him and his descendants forever. Jacob was overwhelmed when he awoke and the awe of God was still there. He said "Surely this is the gate to heaven and I did not know it. It was here that he made a vow to God setting up an altar and calling the place Bethel.

Remember it was a dream, but it impacted him because the dream was vivid, clear, instructional and revelatory and he saw himself there in it. The dream's impact made him build an altar and make a vow.

It appears however that although Jacob was greatly impacted by the dream, he hadn't yet learnt how to speak the language and it would be a number of years before the significance of the dream became apparent.

The next 20 - 25 years passed and Jacob had lots going on in his life. He moved to Haran, fell in love, built a family, worked hard and submitted to another man's house.

Then in Gen 31:13 the Lord appeared and said; "I AM the God of Bethel," now return to the place of the dream, to the place where the promise to you and your descendants was made.

Jacob may have forgotten the dream but God never did, He came saying "I AM the God of Bethel" or IAM the God of the Dream. The point being that the dream had been instrumental in establishing the promises made to Abraham and Isaac that their descendants would possess the land and prosper. Jacob prospered in Haran, if it had not been for the dream he may never have returned to Bethel. Jacob never forgot the language and when he heard it again it triggered him to respond, Jacob now spoke the language.

Dreams & visions are spirit language and God wants you and I to learn the language, so when he speaks to us in this language we have understanding, not just interest or curiosity.

The language of dreams and visions is so intense we sometimes feel like we are actually in the picture, it is my belief that this language of the spirit in fact draws us into the image. We are there.

When I was Pastor of a Church in Auckland a member of that Church had the following experience and he shared his testimony with us.

The man said his dream was so vivid he felt like he had been there. He explained that when he was younger and living in Fiji, he had a friendship with a family who were Muslim. The children loved him and called him Uncle. Almost twenty years had passed since he immigrated to New Zealand and although they had spasmodic contact by phone and letter, the families had not seen each other in that time.

In the dream he saw himself standing at the side of the bed of one of the young women of the family. She was very sick, and in the dream he shared with her how the love of Jesus had changed him and how he had been healed of many injuries received in a car accident. He then shared how Jesus loved her and was very willing to heal her. In the dream she allowed him to pray for her and in the dream she was healed and she

11

came to an understanding of Jesus and the salvation available to her. The dream ended and the man woke thinking about the amazing dream. It was 5am because he glanced at his alarm clock. If this was all that occurred you would say that it was an encouraging dream, but what transpired next was the miracle. At 9am the man received an international phone call from the young woman he had seen in the dream. She was healed; her testimony was that she was chronically ill for 18 months and bedridden for 8 months. Now she was healed and she said she had no way to explain what had happened. She had seen the man standing at her side in the night and praying for her. She had a full understanding of what had happened and that it happened in the name of Jesus. As a result she wanted to accept Jesus as her Saviour. She explained that this was the reason for the phone call. She was able to tell the man exactly what he had said and exactly what had occurred. The Lord had miraculously touched this woman (a Muslim) and transformed her life through a godly man living in another country. This is the power of a godly dream.

The second testimony occurred with me on a recent Saturday night. I had a very vivid dream. In the dream the phone rang and it was a friend on the other end. She told me in the dream she was feeling really low and really needed prayer. In the dream I went to war on her behalf and saw huge objects shifting that were causing her to feel so low. Next morning (Sunday) I sent her an e-mail to encourage her about the dream in which she shared her heart. This is the response I got back.

"What you have shared has truly encouraged me; yes I was in a very low place Saturday and all I could do was lie down and soak in God's presence. It is very encouraging to know that other people will stand in the gap when you can't walk anymore and all you can do is stand...having done all, stand...or lie down as it was!. Thank you for being so open to God and sharing this with me....it truly gives me strength to keep going."

Church history is full of such events, but in this day of reason Christians don't allow the Lord to move in this kind of language. Or if they do acknowledge the vision or dream it's often just communicated as interesting and not taken seriously.

Now is the time to move in the power of the supernatural realm to overcome the works of the evil one. If there are barriers of politics and religion stopping us taking the gospel into areas, then we need to start believing for a release of the power of Godly dreams. Dare to dream Godly dreams and allow Him to use you to change the world. Even if you are confined to your home Jesus can and will, still use you.

The New Testament is full of dreams. In fact in the book of Matthew the birth and safety of Jesus is recorded as involving four dreams.

The first dream; now the birth of Jesus Christ was as follows: After His mother Mary was betrothed to Joseph, before they came together, she was found with child of the Holy Spirit. Then Joseph her husband, being a just man, and not wanting to make her a public example, was minded to put her away secretly. But while he thought about these things, behold, an angel of the Lord appeared to him in a dream, saying, "Joseph, son of David, do not be afraid to take to you Mary your wife, for that which is conceived in her is of the Holy Spirit. And she will bring forth a Son, and you shall call His name Jesus, for He will save His people from their sins." **Matt 1:18-21**

The second dream involved the wise men being divinely warned in a dream that they should not return to Herod, which caused them to depart for their own country another way.
Matt 2:12

The third dream was to Joseph after the wise men had departed, an angel of the Lord appeared to Joseph in a dream, saying, "Arise, take the young Child and His mother, flee to Egypt, and stay there until I bring you word; for Herod will seek the young Child to destroy Him." When he

14

arose, he took the young Child and His mother by night and departed for Egypt. **Matt 2:13-14**

The forth dream also involved Joseph. When Herod was dead, behold, an angel of the Lord appeared in a dream to Joseph in Egypt, saying, "Arise, take the young Child and His mother, and go to the land of Israel, for those who sought the young Child's life are dead." Then he arose, took the young Child and His mother, and came into the land of Israel. **Matt 2:19-21**

So we see that this language of dreams was not foreign to Joseph or others at this time and was taken as a serious instruction from the Lord. Whereas today many would say, "I had an interesting dream" but take no leading or action because of it.

Many dreams are, in fact, not just dreams but become supernatural and actual encounters, such as what happened to Peter in Acts chapter 12.

Acts 12:6-19 (NLT) The night before Peter was to be placed on trial, he was asleep, fastened with two chains between two soldiers. Others stood guard at the prison gate. Suddenly, there was a bright light in the cell, and an angel of the Lord stood before Peter. The angel struck him on the side to awaken him and said, "Quick! Get up!" And the chains fell off his wrists. Then the angel told him, "Get dressed and put on your sandals."

And he did. "Now put on your coat and follow me," the angel ordered. So Peter left the cell, following the angel. But all the time he thought it was a vision. He didn't realize it was actually happening. They passed the first and second guard posts and came to the iron gate leading to the city, and this opened for them all by itself. So they passed through and started walking down the street, and then the angel suddenly left him. Peter finally came to his senses. "It's really true!" he said. "The Lord has sent his angel and saved me from Herod and from what the Jewish leaders had planned to do to me!" When he realized this, he went to the home of Mary, the mother of John Mark, where many were gathered for prayer. He knocked at the door in the gate, and a servant girl named Rhoda came to open it. When she recognized Peter's voice, she was so overjoyed that, instead of opening the door, she ran back inside and told everyone, "Peter is standing at the door!" "You're out of your mind!" they said. When she insisted, they decided, "It must be his angel." Meanwhile, Peter continued knocking. When they finally opened the door and saw him, they were amazed. He motioned for them to quiet down and told them how the Lord had led him out of prison. "Tell James and the other brothers what happened," he said. And then he went to another place. At dawn there was a great commotion among the soldiers about what had happened to Peter. Herod Agrippa ordered a thorough search for him. When he couldn't be found, Herod interrogated the guards and sentenced them to death. Afterward Herod left Judea to stay in Caesarea for a while.

The striking thing about this scripture is that what starts as a dream ends in Peter being translated into the middle of the street. Let's take a close look at what the scripture in Acts 12 is telling us.

1) There were guards every where, in the cell, at the doors, by the gate.
2) It was dark until the Angel lit up the whole room; no guards noticed.
3) The Angel dug Peter in the ribs, he would have woken with a start and a noise, if it hadn't been a dream; again no guards notice.
4) Metal Chains fall off onto rock floor, no guards notice.
5) Peter puts his clothes and shoes on, no guards notice.
6) They go through three sets of gates and three sets of guards, no one notices.
7) Peter thinks is this real or is it a dream?
8) Peter comes to him self (wakes up) and he's in the middle of the street.

What started as a vivid dream became Peter's reality because Peter became totally engaged in the language being spoken by the spirit in the dream and as a result was translated to the middle of the road and awoke.

NOTES

NOTES:

PART 2 – VISIONS.

We have covered dreams in the previous chapter and in this Chapter we will look at the broader realm of visions, which also include the realm of dreams.

There are various Greek words which describe the types of vision recorded in the New Testament. These are the Languages of the Holy Spirit. The important thing to remember is that there are many languages but only one speaker and that is the Holy Spirit.

The words used to describe this language of the Holy Spirit are as follows:

1) Onar - Dream
This is the word most often used for dream which we have already covered.

2) Enupnion – Night Visions.
Also a vision received while asleep but specifically spiritual in nature and clearly instructional and not metaphoric in nature.

One time Jesus came to me in a dream and took me onto the landing of our house, there we spoke, He asked me to do something very specific and then asked me, Will you do this for me? I thought in the dream, how do you say no to Jesus? So I said yes, but what Jesus was asking me to do affected my wife, so I said Lord will you tell Joye because I am going to need her with me on this. He said sure and we went to Joye who was sleeping and I woke her in the dream and said, "Joye, Jesus wants to speak to you" she said "I'm sleeping what does he want?" Her response made Jesus laugh, he just said "Hello Joye." Now next morning when I related the dream to Joye, it triggered a response in her and she was able to accept the request of Jesus. She had the impression in her heart of having had a real encounter with Jesus. The response of Jesus to her in the dream was the Jesus she knows and loves. I would say that this experience was "Enupnion" or Night Visions.

3) Horama – open vision. You are awake and most often have your eyes open.

Instances of this are; Matt 17:9 Peter, James and John see Jesus Transfigured.
Acts 9:10-12 Ananias receives instructions about Saul (Paul)
Acts 10:3-4 Cornelius receives instructions from an Angel
Acts 16:9-10 Paul's Macedonian vision to come and preach.

This kind of vision is in real time and you are able to interact in it and hear and see everything, because you are part of the vision.

Once I found myself in Sierra Leone which is a place I have never been, yet I am able to describe the place as clear as if I was still standing there now. I was ministering to people and they were responding. I heard someone say that the place was called Lungi, Id never heard of it, yet I know that is where we were. When I had returned I looked up the name Lungi, its near Freetown close to the airport. I didn't know that because in the natural I've never been to Sierra Leone, but in the Horama vision, I was there.

4) Optasia – Apparition; you see it but it's ethereal.

New Testament examples of this are;
Zechariah the father of John the Baptist when he sees the Angel of the Lord in Luke 1:22.

Luke 24:22-23 – gives a description of the angels at the tomb of Jesus by the woman who were there.

In 2 Cor 12:1-4 Paul describes the visions the Lord has given him.

This Optasia realm is the one I have experienced most regularly, where out of nowhere an apparition comes.

Once when I was speaking in a meeting the whole back of the room, opened and another realm became visible, beings moved out of the torn veil and into the room, people began to fall off their seats as the atmosphere of Heaven came. I heard the beings, giving me encouragement to keep preaching and the atmosphere became electric.

Most of my Angelic encounters have been in this form. Once at the end of a series of meetings, as can often happen when you've seen some major breakthroughs, I felt a little low. I prayed and asked the Lord, "Did the meetings really make a difference?" Then that same evening, I awoke from my sleep to see an apparition of an angel before me. He was large and had glowing features, he had a white sash with the blue Star of David on it, he spoke and said I have come from Jerusalem to tell you that your words have been heard on the walls of the city and they have made a difference. That was the answer to my question, God sent his angel to encourage me.

5) Ekstasis – Ecstasy (Trance) awake usually eyes closed and sometimes frozen on the spot. New Testament examples are;
Acts 10:10 Peter on the roof top.
Acts 22:17 Paul falls into a trance and receives instructions.

In a meeting with Kathie Walters I first stepped into this trance vision state. I have seen past present and future events, in this way. Often if I

am in a meeting I will go and sit against a wall and become frozen on the spot. Most often I am taken into encounter or instructional vision.
 I once had a past encounter with the apostle Phillip. I saw his crucifixion in what is now modern day Turkey. I saw it all and I also saw where they buried him. That was in 2009. In 2010 they discovered a tomb in that place with inscriptions that would suggest it was the resting place of Phillip. I know it is because I was there in a trance vision.

Once I was taken over much of New Zealand and many future events were shown to me, I have written a lot over the past few years based on that encounter. Much of what I have seen and declared has come to pass.

6) Apokalupsis – Inner vision or revelation. Picture, or words scrolling but its inward.

Eph 1:17 The Lord grant you a spirit of wisdom and revelation - Galatians 2:2

Often while speaking to someone or preaching the words just scroll in my spirit and I find myself answering questions or saying something that I don't really know about. Afterwards as I checked out what was said, it proved correct based on the word. I love the way the Lord can do this.

7) Pneumati – you are caught into another place in the spirit but fully aware of what's going on. You are translated into another realm the realm of the Spirit.

A New Testament example; Rev 1:9-10 John caught up into heaven.

Many times I find myself in heavenly encounters or places, as well as in various countries I have never been to, being instructed or being used in some way to release the will of God. I have no explanation for some of the things I have done or places I have been in the spirit. I can't get there on my own. The Lord opens up a realm and I step into it. This is what John called being in the Spirit.

So, however the Lord chooses to reveal Himself or His instructions, it should always lead us into fellowship with Christ or a revelation of His purposes. Our home is in Him; therefore our view in Him is from the place where he is seated, in heavenly places. I am in Him and He is in me. There are no restrictions in Him, as He sees, so I can see.

Eph 2:6 says; for He raised us from the dead along with Christ, and we are seated with Him in the heavenly realms—all because we are one with Christ Jesus.

As we then come into the fullness of being seated with Christ, the view from Heaven changes our mindsets and is a trigger for the miraculous and revival in our hearts to those we speak to.

We are called to enter into the presence of God; not just to experience a tingly feeling down our spine as He passes by, or goose bumps as we catch a glimpse of Him through the veil. But we are called to enter into the realm of the Spirit and to see from a heavenly perspective; to literally be in Him.

Jesus was operating from a heavenly perspective all the time; for instance when he called Nathaniel; (John 2:47-51) Jesus said "I saw you under a fig tree." Where did he see him?
He was seeing Nathaniel and his heart not as men see, that is from an earthly perspective but He saw him in some sort of vision.

The same with the story of Lazarus (John 11). Jesus wasn't hurried or fazed by the circumstance, because He had seen the event from heaven's perspective. Again we are not told how.

In verse 40 he says "Did I not say to you that if you would believe you would see the glory of God?"

All the miracles Jesus performed He first saw from heaven's perspective, and when He spoke He only spoke what He heard or had seen from heaven's perspective.

Isaiah 48:3 "I have declared the former things from the beginning; they went forth from my mouth, and I caused them to hear it. Suddenly I did them, and they came to pass."

By faith, we need to see ourselves in heavenly places; and when you do, you will be there in a dream, various forms of vision or in the spirit. You will hear what the father says, you will see the end and the beginning of an issue and your spiritual life will change forever.

The plan of the enemy is to keep the people of God earth bound and blind to the things of the Spirit through religious mindsets and arguments of, and agreement with, the flesh. It so saddens me to hear people say that they don't want to enter into the realms of the Spirit, into that place of standing in Heaven with Jesus, of seeing the Earth from the perspective of Heaven, because they are afraid of the spiritual. If you are in Christ, then your home is in the supernatural realm of Heaven with Christ. You are in the world, but not of the world.

The reformation in 1514 was essentially a German one and there wasn't any room for the mystical side of the Catholic Church that the likes of Francis Xavier and Ignatius Loyola and countless other mystics exhibited in their lives. You can change your world today as you choose to rise into heavenly places and let the Glory invade your thinking. God is causing a people to rise up and to tear down mindsets. This is the season to enter into the language of the Holy Spirit.

NOTES

WORKING WITH ANGELS

WORKING WITH ANGELS.

ANGELS; Even the mention of the word seems to bring a shiver up the collective back of much of the body of Christ. To me there is almost nothing more biblical than angels.

Angels are mentioned three hundred and seventy five times in the Bible, more than love, gospel, or peace. 33% in the Old Testament; 67% in the New. So you can't even say that angels are an Old Testament thing.

My first Pastor said to me that if something was mentioned once in the Bible it was important, twice very important and more than three times, extremely important and we ignore at our peril. So it seems to me that if something is mentioned three hundred and seventy five times it is important to the furthering of the Kingdom.

People often say "The Bible says you shouldn't talk to Angels," and I say if you can find a scripture to back that statement up, then forty eight individuals that I've found listed in the Bible, from Genesis to Revelation who have had conversations with Angels, must be in the wrong book.

The Bible is clear we shouldn't worship Angels and it seems to me that if an Angel came into the room and asked to be worshiped or didn't pick you up and say "get up for I am a servant of the Lord just as you are and the Lord alone is due our worship," then I think you would know he was not from God.

Gal 1:8-9, Let God's curse fall on anyone, including myself, who preaches any other message than the one we told you about. Even if an angel comes from heaven and preaches any other message, let him be forever cursed. I will say it again: If anyone preaches any other gospel than the one you welcomed, let God's curse fall upon that person.

Paul in no uncertain terms made it clear that any messages received from God's Angels would always bring glory to the Lord and line up with a gospel of reconciliation through Jesus Christ.

2 Cor 11:14-15, Even Satan can disguise himself as an angel of light. So it is no wonder his servants can also do it by pretending to be godly ministers. In the end they will get every bit of punishment their wicked deeds deserve.

The likes of Mohammad and Joseph Smith were deceived by an Angel of light and introduced a new false doctrine. If scripture had been followed this would not have been possible. Neither "Gospel" honours Jesus Christ as God and therefore cannot be of God. It should be said that any Angel that preaches any message outside that which was preached by the Apostles is False. Any Angel that seeks worship is false; the true Angels of God will rebuke us the moment we even try. Any Angel that won't confess that Jesus Christ came in the flesh and is man's only hope of salvation is false. So there are plenty of ways to test the Spirits. The Angel that came to Joseph Smith was introducing a new Gospel of salvation where Jesus was seen as just a man. That should tell you something. The Angels that come to New Age worshipers will not accept that Jesus is the only way of Salvation; that should tell you something. The Angel that came to Mohammad said that Jesus was just one in a long line of Prophets but that Mohammad was the last and true prophet; that should tell you something!

The only danger is if we are prideful and puffed up about talking to angels, it would indicate that we are building our Kingdom and not the Lords. It's not so hard to spot the deception if we walk in humility. Remember there is one Gospel and only one way to God and that is through Jesus Christ, who is God. No Angel will receive worship if they are from God.

So before I tell you of some Angels I've met I need to show you the biblical basis for talking with Angels or seeing Angels to help us understand why in this Age we need to, more than ever, look for the assistance of the Angelic host.

1) There are lots of them; Revelation 5:11 says 10,000 x 10,000 and thousands of thousands. Well 10,000 x 10,000 is a Billion; so with that description we can figure there are several Billion! Jesus said he could have asked for 12 legions of Angels to come to his aid if he desired, A legion is 6000, so Jesus had 72,000 Angels immediately at his call.

2) The Greek word "Angelos" translated Angels, simply means Messengers.

3) Angels are created beings and were created before the creation of the world; Job 38:4-7, Col 1:16. How long before? We are not told, but we can assume they have been around for a long time.

4) They are Spirits Heb 1:14, Psalm 104:4. Spirits; who do not have a body like men, although they can take on the likeness and appearance of men.

5) They are subject to Jesus; Heb 1:4-6. Jesus is the Lord of Hosts, who are the hosts? The angels and the saints. Jesus is Lord of all.

6) They have powers of discernment; 2 Sam 14:17-20. Angels exhibit a high level of intelligence and reflect the nature of God but are not as smart as God. They are not omniscient, or omnipresent.

7) They were created holy; Mark 8:38. YHVH is the creator of all things and out of Himself he created everything that exists, including Angels and heavenly beings.

8) They have a high level of wisdom; Heb 2:7, but much lower than God; Heb 1:4.

9) They can have an awesome appearance Luke 1:11; Several times when an Angel appeared his first words were "Fear not". Angels that come into this realm from the throne room reflect the glory of God, so their appearance is glorious, it's not their glory but Gods glory reflected.

10) They are attentive to the Father for instruction; Matt 18:10. Always wanting to act out and fulfill the Father's desires and will they are attentive to Him.

11) There are Angels assigned to individuals; Matt 18:10. Every person has an angel assigned to them. Some have many depending on their calling. This can vary from assignment to assignment. On our first trip to Israel the Lord told my wife, Joye that He had assigned extra angles to travel with us, and help us with the ministry there.

12) They are generally invisible but can become visible and eat food; Luke 2:9. They are only invisible in the natural realm.

13) Angels are strong. One killed 185,000 Assyrians (2 Kings 19:35) and one slew 70,000 Israelites (2 Sam 24:15-16.)

14) Angels never die; Luke 20:35-36. God created them to reflect his eternal nature

15) They have various names. Watchers, Holy ones, Holy Angels, Hosts, Sons of God, Sons of the Mighty, Elect of God, ministering Spirits, Messengers, Angel of the Church, Guardians, Guardian Angels, Warriors and flaming fire.

What do Angels do?

1) Called to worship God. Rev 5:11-12 , Rev 8:3-4

2) Called to protect the saints. Matt 4:11, Dan 6:22

3) They lead Christians to the unsaved and unsaved to Christians. Acts 8:26 , Acts 10:30-32

4) Look after children. Matt 18:10

5) Protect people. Dan 6:22

6) Announce God's plans. Luke 2:13

7) Look into the affairs of men. 1 Pet 1:12

8) Help to see the will of God performed in the earth. Num 22:22 Balaam, Herod's demise. Acts 12:23

9) Take the Lord's people home at death. Luke 16:22

10) Encamp around those that fear the Lord. Psalm 34:7

11) Form the Lords army. Mat 16:22-27

12) Help reap the end time harvest. Matt 13:39

The Bible says we should entertain strangers because we never know when we are entertaining Angels unaware, Hebrews 13:2. This tells us that God expects us to expect Angels in our life. They are there to help us, and when someone gets saved the Angels rejoice, Luke 15:7.

In the Scripture there is a long list of interventions by Angels; in fact I've found forty eight instances of two way conversations with Angels. In many cases the course of human history has changed forever because of these interventions. However, never has the spotlight been taken off the Father, Jesus or the Holy Spirit, by any of these interventions. Some of the Angelic encounters are quite different experiences, like Balaam's Donkey or Elisha's servant but in all cases there is a victory for the true and living God.

Here are just a few of those who spoke to Angels or to whom Angels spoke. Hagar, Abraham, Isaac, Jacob, Lot ,Moses, Balaam's Donkey, Balaam, Joshua, All the Children of Israel in Judges 2:1-6, Gideon, Elijah , Elisha Angels & Horsemen, David, Daniel, Zechariah the Prophet, Elizabeth, Zechariah Father of John the Baptist, Mary, Joseph, Jesus, Shepherds, Wise men, Peter , John, Phillip, Stephen, Paul, The Women at the tomb, Cornelius All the Disciples when Jesus ascended. Concerning angels, do your own study, sometimes it will surprise you.

I have had a number of experiences with Angels and there are millions of stories of Angelic activity in the Church right through the Ages and ever more so in this final hour of history. At times of great Godly outpouring in the earth, there is always an influx of angelic activity reported.

Angels are called to protect you. Psalm 91:11, for he orders his angels to protect you wherever you go. They will hold you with their hands to keep you from striking your foot on a stone.

Psalm 34:7, for the angel of the Lord guards all who fear him, and he rescues them.

God's Angels are on your side and its time to take hold of the supernatural realm and live in it. Kathie Walters always says. The Supernatural, the chariots and the Angels are meant to be a normal part of every Christian, life.

There was an evangelist in NZ many years ago called Bob Kingi, he had lots of Angel stories, but the one I loved the most was when he was ministering in Australia. The Lord moved powerfully in the morning service and there were many miracles, signs and wonders, but Bob was very late finishing, in fact there was no way he would make it to the night meeting several hours drive away. Bob thought to cancel the night meeting but the Holy Spirit compelled him to set out in his car. About 30 minutes into his journey Bob saw a hitch hiker and decided to pick him up. When he took his back pack to put in the boot Bob noticed it was very light in fact it seemed empty, but he thought nothing of it. On the journey the man started to talk to Bob about the wonders of the Lord, and all track of time was lost. Suddenly the man said this is where I get out Bob said, there's nothing here we are in the middle of nowhere, but the man insisted, so Bob let him out. The man blessed bob in the name of the Lord and Bob drove off. Looking in his rear view mirror there was no sign of his passenger, within five minutes Bob arrived in the town he was due to speak at in the evening. He looked at his watch and realised he had fifteen minutes to spare before the meeting began. The five hour journey had only taken one and a half hours to complete. His passenger had to be an Angel.

Bob and his car had been translated in time. Did Bob become deceived by this experience? Not at all. Up until the time of his death, he preached the Gospel of Jesus.

I once knew a Christian Traffic officer who found himself in a very difficult situation one night with a group of thugs. The ugly men were coming towards him with pipes and knives and meant to do a lot of damage to him. Suddenly they just turned and ran. Later the men were arrested on another matter and the traffic officer was curious to know why they had run. They told him it was because of the five big men who stepped out of his car and started moving toward them. Angels! Did this situation deceive my friend, not at all, it encouraged his faith and he became a Pastor.

In 2004 and 2005 I was uplifted in the spirit by an Angel & Chariot at meetings being conducted by Kathie Walters in New Zealand and Australia. The first time, I was shown several nations and taken to the western wall in Jerusalem. There I was given orders and a commissioning to Israel & the nations we had visited. In 2004 – 2007 it felt in the natural that what I had seen was just a dream. During those years we went through very hard times and it seemed impossible that I would ever see some of these nations. Then In March 2008 an Angel of Breakthrough came to me in a meeting and declared "Breakthrough." Since that time I have visited Australia, Israel, Malaysia, Singapore, India, Portugal and Turkey, doors of ministry have opened in other places I visited on that journey of instruction and commissioning.

Have these visitations (and there now have been many) taken me away from the call to take the gospel and spread the glory of His Kingdom to the nations? No! it has increased 1000 fold and my love for Jesus and his glory in the earth has increased, my abandonment to the Father and my hunger for the Holy Spirit have been fuelled by these visitations.

If we close our lives to the work of Angels we miss a big part of what God wants to do with us! My feeling is, that if we want to see the results that the early Church saw and we want to see multitudes saved, if our desire is to see the will of God fulfilled in the world, and we want to remain safe doing it, then we are going to have to work with the Angels to see the work done. The Church was born in supernatural power by the God of Israel who has always demonstrated to the Jewish people that they have lots of help through Angelic intervention.

Each one of you have at least one Angel who works on your behalf, if you are in Ministry you will have several. I know of four who work with me when I'm ministering each has a different function and I very seldom make mention of them, because their desire, like mine, is to see Jesus glorified, but they are there and work with me at the command of the Father.

Each Church that is ordained of God will have an Angel assigned to it. They are so passionate about protecting the Church they are assigned to they will block anything that is not sanctioned by the Church leaders. The Lord allowed me to see this when I was ministering in Perth Western Australia. The Pastor didn't introduce me but just said to me just get up and go for it. Well I was allowed to see the Church Angel and he wouldn't stand aside and let my ministering Angels come forward. I said to the Pastor "do you mind just introducing me and welcoming me into the Church"? This he did and immediately the Church Angel stood back and my ministering Angels came forward. We had an amazing move of God but if we hadn't done that, things would have been tough. I was in another Church one time when a prophetic anointing came on me and I began to declare what I was seeing for the Church. The Angel of the Church got so excited that he began to slap me on the back in encouragement. Now every one wondered why I was making sudden moves to the left and the right, it was just an excited Church Angel.

Don't be afraid of the Angelic realm. Don't fall into the trap of blocking out the Angelic help available to you and your ministry. The Father won't give you a stone if you ask for bread, or He won't give you a scorpion if you ask for a fish. Sure there are bad Angels around who work for the Devil, but the good news is that there are two thirds of all the Angels on your side and they really want to help us see Jesus the King and His Kingdom established.

As we enter the last days we are going to see an outpouring of the supernatural because God is a supernatural God who lives in a supernatural place and does supernatural things. The new age folk are more used to seeing into the supernatural than the Church, and that's not how it's meant to be. Don't allow the fear of deception to cause you to throw the baby out with the bath water.

The encounters you have may seem just like a dream at first like Peter, who we saw in the dream session when the Angel broke him out of prison. Peter understood that it wasn't a dream when he was half way across the street and totally out of prison.

Some of you have had experiences just like that and have dismissed it. When I first went in a

Chariot it took an act of faith on my part to step into the chariot. But the moment I stepped out in faith, I was in the vision with the Angelic messenger, and the start of a whole new ministry to the nations opened up before me.

Angels have been commanded to help you bring the Gospel of Jesus Christ to a dying world, they won't step in to preach the Gospel, that's our job, but they will give you lots of help along the way. There's a whole new world waiting for you to walk into. Ask the Lord to show you the help you have with you; you may even have an experience like that of Elisha's servant, where God opened his eyes to see the warring angels that were on their side.

NOTES

NOTES

MOTIVATION OF THE HEART

AND

PROPHETIC INTERCESSION

MOTIVATION OF THE HEART & PROPHETIC INTERCESSION

I Love the following quote by the Kingdom son Bono from U2. "The Lord's prayer says As it is in Heaven so also on earth - So stop asking God to bless what you do, instead find out what God is already doing because that is already blessed."

In this statement lies the understanding of what true intercession is. It is finding out what God is doing and agreeing with Him. Jesus prayed and lived like this. He only ever did what he heard the Father say, or he only ever did what the Holy Spirit had shown him in Heaven.

We must allow the increase of His presence to be so absorbed into our spirits that we not only believe in Him, we believe like Him. His love, thoughts and desires flow out from within us as naturally as fruit appear on a vine.

Prophetic intercession is a declaration of what you see in heaven being released on earth, no more, no less. We are called to declare what we see, then allow the Lord to bring substance to our seeing by stepping back and allowing God to bring the answer. One of the big mistakes prophetic intercessors make is thinking that they have to make it happen, when the truth is we have to allow Him to make it happen.

God is calling us to renew the apostolic/prophetic foundation of our faith and to move out of the soul and into a realm that is measured by the impact and reality of the spiritual realm.

To see the joy on a face when Heaven's door rolls open and the scene is revealed is just about as good as seeing it yourself. God is calling you to see what he sees and then declare it.
It's like fragrance that suddenly triggers the memory of a dream or wind that cools summer's air. It burns in your heart and thirsts in your soul till you long to see the door yourself. When that person hears the sounds of Heaven and releases them into this world it's like your whole being is captured by waves of glory, passion for the eternal realm is stirred and worship for the King is released.

This door builds faith and the sights and sounds of Heaven revealed become substance in earth's realms, when you declare what you have seen. Just as it says in the book of Hebrews chapter 11 "Faith is the substance of things hoped for and the evidence of things unseen." So a glimpse into Heaven needs to be released through testimony or declaration in order to gain the substance of the unseen in this realm.

Prophetic utterances are not just a few good words that come out of the soul of man, rather they are a release of substance that has been seen in the spiritual realm and then spoken into the earthly realm. The vision has moved from unseen to seen by the release of our testimony. "The testimony of Jesus is the Spirit of prophecy."

All prophecy recorded in the Bible came from a revelation of the unseen realm; such as Ezekiel's word in chapter 37 where the Lord says to him "Son of man can these bones live?" What bones? The bones that he had seen when he was carried in the Spirit and set down in the midst of them. Ezekiel was there, it wasn't a picture or a feeling he was carried and set down in the midst. What he saw and heard he recorded and it became substance.

Gentiles are in the kingdom today because in Acts 10, Peter in a trance, saw into another realm; he saw clean and unclean animals and plants on a sheet, the Lord said, "Peter take and eat" but Peter said "No Lord for I have never eaten unclean things." The Lord replied, "That which I call clean is clean." Peter chose to release that which he had seen and heard in the unseen realm into this realm by speaking it to Cornelius and his household and to the Gentiles, the glory of that one encounter endures to this day.

The importance of prophetic intercession transcends time and brings eternity into this realm. The Holy Spirit wants to encourage you to seek Jesus where He is, which is in the unseen realm of Heaven and then when He reveals Himself in your spirit, we are called to release what we see into this realm, the earth or the seen realm.

It is time for the Church to enter into this level of the prophetic intercession again and move out of soulish immaturity. This is true Prophetic intercession and the very foundation of the church.

This is a season to move out of the council of men where the realm of the soul reigns and move into the foundation of the apostles; (Jesus being the chief among them) where the spirit reigns. That which comes out of the soul sounds good because it stimulates the soul; but we must move beyond our soul into a zone that is uncomfortable to the soul and release the true spirit of prophecy.

The outcome of such a prophetic revelation is; "Heaven released." It has substance it is not ethereal or flaky, it is a transforming glory, it is the Kingdom released on earth as it is in heaven.

HOW BIG IS JESUS IN YOUR PRAYER WORLD?
If your life is a battle trying to break through with prayer and if in your intercession all you see is the battle, - chances are Jesus is not the centre of your prayer. The need becomes bigger than the answer. True intercession is finding out what God

is saying in a given situation, then agreeing with Him. That way the battle is the Lords and we are victorious in HIM. Every answer to prayer is His victory not our victory, but In Him we get to enjoy the fruit. When we warfare from a place of victory in Him, our warfare becomes joyous and full of jubilation, not striving.

Intercessory prayer must never be directional; to see our will fulfilled, but must always be in agreement with HIS will. Directional prayer towards a person is paramount to witchcraft and causes huge disruption in the spiritual realm. Jesus never did anything thing unless He first heard the Father speak it. We are called to walk the same way, to hear/see God's purpose and agree with Him by declaring what we see and hear.

Agreement with the will of God is not blindly quoting scripture, it's agreeing with the scripture revealed or the vision revealed, or the dream revealed – Finding the will of God is seeing through HIS heart in any given matter and agreeing with HIM.

When we speak we are called to speak out of the atmosphere of Heaven which is full of glory not out of an earthly perspective. The position you speak from is important. Heaven or Earth, your perspective or His.

When you speak from heaven you speak from an eternal point of view, so time is irrelevant - Seeing from a heavenly (Eternal) perspective you see as God sees. It changes the way you pray from a demand to an agreement. This type of prayer becomes very exciting because outside of Him we have no idea how the answer will come. We can't rely on our abilities but must cast ourselves on His. We truly become the body of Christ when we exercise the mind and will of Christ in this type of agreement with Him.

Christ is the visible image of the invisible God. He existed before anything was created and is supreme over all creation; for through Him God created everything in the heavenly realms and on earth. He made the things we can see and the things we can't see— such as thrones, kingdoms, rulers, and authorities in the unseen world. Everything was created through him and for him. He existed before anything else, and he holds all creation together. Col 1:15-17 (NLT.)

Before we enter into the realm of agreement with God we need to get the motivation of our heart in order. Our motivational calling is to walk in the mind of Christ. To see as God sees.

Sometimes we feel a subtle blocking by our friends, relations, or brothers and sisters in the faith. We feel and see the right words, but know it is the wrong motivation.

Jesus himself said "I judge not after the flesh but after the heart".

In order to have the mind of Christ in any situation, including prayer, we need to discern by the motivation of the heart

There are four voices that affect our motivation

1) The Holy Spirit's language.
2) Our human spirit's language.
3) Our human soul's language.
4) Our flesh language.

The Holy Spirit's communication triggers are
Dreams
Visions
Revelations
Emotions/ Thoughts
Comfort/discomfort

Gifts to bring life out of Heaven are often dismissed because of mind sets which are driven by our hearts motivations. We become stuck in religion, or fear because we won't allow the Holy Spirit to trigger the languages of Heaven. Discerning our own and others motivation helps us see the nature of that which is veiled.

The question we need to ask is; where is my thinking in intercession coming from?

Holy Spirit?
Good Angels?
Fallen Angels?
Human Spirits?

Mind sets/motivations make us suspicious of
anything unseen by the natural eyes but we need
to discern all things including the motivation of
the heart. The way we clean up our motivation is
by submitting everything to the Spirit of truth.
Trusting that the spirit of truth will lead us into
all truth.

Jesus was totally effective in his ministry because
he didn't make assumptions in his intercession.
He walked in total obedience to the Father.

We walk by faith and we are told that without
faith it is impossible to please God. Our faith will
only go as far as our mindsets will allow it to go.
So the most important part of becoming an
effective Kingdom son or daughter in the area of
intercession is, constantly submitting our
mindsets to the Spirit of truth, and being open to
the language of the spirit.

We are called to transform the world, to bring
Heaven to earth and to establish His Kingdom.
To do this, intercession needs to change to align
with heaven. Prayer meetings never need to be
the same again.

NOTES

NOTES

KINGDOM
FATHERS

HEAVENS SONS

Kingdom Fathers – Heavens Sons

When I was in Turkey in 2009, I went to Ephesus the once great city where the gospel went out to the known world. Nearby are the ruins of a first century Church where it is believed that John the Apostle was buried. Tradition has it that John, on his return from exile on the Island of Patmos, was taken back to his beloved Ephesus where he lived as a very old man. No one knows how old John was but we do know that Jesus told John he would be the only one of the twelve to die of old age. Tradition says that John was so full of love that even though speech had abandoned him in his last days, they would carry him into the Church altar and soak up the power of Jesus's love that permeated John's frail frame. The writings of John back up this tradition. He wrote; "See how very much our Father loves us, for he calls us his children, and that is what we are! But the people who belong to this world don't recognize that we are God's children because they don't know him. Dear friends, we are already God's children, but he has not yet shown us what we will be like when Christ appears. But we do know that we will be like him, for we will see him as he really is" 1 John 3:1-2 (NLT)

John was a true Father of thousands when he
wrote that. He had lived a life of abandonment
that led him into the courts of the true Father. In
his own life he reflected his heavenly Father's
heart. John was a true Elder who released Heaven
on earth.

In Hebrew culture the elders ruled from the gates
of a city. Jesus became a gate for us into another
realm and in his possession of us we become a
gate for him into this realm. John was a gate of
love, a gate where the perfect love of God
expelled all fear. We are called in the same way
and into the same gates.

In the Bible it talks about Samuel sitting in the
gate, all the judges of Israel are recorded as
judging in the gate. David and Solomon sat in the
gate to make decisions. Gates are important.

Fathers and Mothers sit in the gates and guard the
way for others to come and go freely into the
presence of God. Currently there aren't enough
Fathers sitting in the gates of the Church.
Fathers, who have walked in and partaken of the
suffering and victories of Christ. Fathers who
have laid down their lives for the King. So as a
result the gates are polluted and the judgement
that flows from the gates is the wisdom of men
and not that of the King.

Fathers and Mothers of the faith, it's time to arise and possess the gates - Sons can't learn obedience while Fathers neglect the gates. You can't open a gate you don't possess or have allowed others to possess on your behalf.

There is no issue over ownership; the King owns the gates and Fathers possess them on His behalf. The alternative is to allow the gates to be possessed by invaders through neglect. For Sons to be released and feel fulfilled they need Fathers to open the gates. So arise Fathers and fulfil your destiny.

Fathers who sit in the gate have the authority to make decisions that affect Sons. But Fathers also carry the weight of responsibility to exercise the Kings wishes towards the Sons. They are not called to exercise their own wishes or desires, but the wishes and desires of the King.

De-facto Fathers often don't hold the same level of commitment to the Sons and often pay no heed to the King's wishes and the Sons suffer. Being a Father is not a career but a calling. Those who see being a Father as a career don't exercise the correct heart towards the Sons and therefore don't hold their highest good as a priority. Fathers don't shut the gates and leave the Sons outside to defend themselves, but maintain a watch always in the Gate.

We are entering an age which is not made up of men and women who claim to be Apostles and demand gold and glory. Rather, the gates are about to be possessed by men and women, Fathers and Mothers, sons and daughters who love like Jesus loved. Jesus revealed the heart of the Father to all God's sons and daughters. The call is not for Fathers and Mothers to decide what can and can't come in through the gate, it is the role of these Fathers and Mothers to teach the sons and daughters how to become the gate.

If someone says, "I love God," but hates a Christian brother or sister, that person is a liar; for if we don't love people we can see, how can we love God, whom we cannot see? And he has given us this command: Those who love God must also love their Christian brothers and sisters. Everyone who believes that Jesus is the Christ has become a child of God. And everyone who loves the Father loves his children, too. 1 John 4:20- 5:1 (NLT.)

So here in this scripture is the test for true apostolic vision; it is love. The love of a Father.

God is not restricted by man's understanding of His word; but He is restricted by His own Character and nature. He will not deviate from this character. So to interoperate His word correctly we need to know His Character and nature.

Intimacy and abandonment through Jesus by the Holy Spirit and towards the Father is the only way we will ever know Him. If we know Him only through His word He will only ever be seen by us as distant, unseen, not as Daddy. To become Sons and Daughters we yield to the Spirit of truth; for those who are led by the Spirit of God are Sons and not slaves. Slaves have no options and can ask no questions; but Sons can reason and ask questions in order to know the Father's heart on a matter.

True apostolic Christianity is driven by encounters and revelations from the Spirit of truth.

Fathers and Mothers are not called to be gatekeepers but gate openers, ones who reveal that the gate into the eternal realm is Jesus, and that the gate from the eternal realm into the earth is through us.

Our understanding of what apostolic Christianity really looks like has been blurred by gatekeepers.

The Apostolic draws us into Sonship; trains us to draw others and releases the Kingdom of God on earth as it is in Heaven, so that all His Sons and Daughters exercise the character and nature of God through intimacy with Him, not just a select elite.

The Apostolic releases the government of God; which is not to keep Sons and Daughters in bondage but to see individuals exercise governmental authority to the world and in the marketplace which releases the will and good pleasure of the Father on Earth. This government shares the way into the king's courts and keeps the enemy out of the gates. When true apostolic government is being exercised the natural government begins to line up.

When gates are opened by the Fathers and Mothers of the faith, the wisdom of the King flows out and Sons and Daughters come to enquire at the gate and show honour. But when the Fathers and Mothers neglect the gates and hold the King's wisdom for themselves the Sons and Daughters follow their own wisdom and stumble.

The Apostolic reformation of the body of Christ is based on encounters with the character and nature of God by virtue of Sonship and inheritance of our Father's nature through covenant. These and not the council of men usher in the Kingdom of God on earth as it is in heaven. Leadership who withhold revelation whilst acting as gatekeepers are not reflecting the true nature of the apostolic.

The Christian faith is about relationship, it's not about religion or outward displays of Church life that are just mere forms and religious expressions. Jesus spoke very firmly to the religious of the day, who felt they were doing the right thing in preserving religious traditions but ignoring its core values. They didn't have the heart of a Father; rather they saw themselves as rulers and gatekeepers.

Soul food that is filling the Church is just junk food in expensive wrappers. Its food not delivered by Fathers and Mothers but by marketers who care little for the Sons and Daughters or the gates. Men and Women who would close a church down because it's in a poor area are not guarding the gate on behalf of the King but are acting as self important gate keepers. If we are to return to true Apostolic government we must return to seeing true Fathers who open wide the gate. The gate must be opened so that the King of Glory may come in to fellowship with Sons and Daughters and to rule over the affairs of men.

Psalms 24:7-10 (ASV)

Lift up your heads, O you gates; and be lifted up, you everlasting doors: And the King of glory will come in. Who is the King of glory? The Lord strong and mighty, The Lord mighty in battle. Lift up your heads, O you gates; Yes, lift them up, you everlasting doors: And the King of glory will come in. Who is this King of glory? The Lord of hosts, He is the King of glory. Selah -

NOTES

BORDERS
AND
GATES

BORDERS AND GATES

In 2009 in Israel I observed an interesting event. We were in the Eilat area; you could see a reasonable amount of the border between Israel and Jordan from where we were. President Obama had just been putting some pressure on Jordan regards the border (with the Palestinian territories).

In Jordan, on the same day a huge dust storm arose. The unusual thing about this storm is that it defined the border between Jordan and Israel, the air was crystal clear on the Israeli side so it formed a line right along the border and out into the Red sea, also defining Israeli territory in the water beyond Saudi Arabia. The Lord was making it clear where he saw the boarders of Israel. It was a miracle and it got me thinking about Borders, Boundaries and Gates.

The scriptures below plainly declares who sets the borders of nations

DEUT 32:8 (NLT); When the Most High assigned lands to the nations, when he divided up the human race; he established the boundaries of the peoples according to the number of angelic beings.

ACTS 17:24; from one man he created all the nations throughout the whole earth. He decided beforehand which should rise and fall and he determined their boundaries.

I've also been pondering the absolute necessity for obedience which opens gates or portals into the realm of Heaven. The opposite is also true, that disobedience opens portals into the enemy's realm. I saw a good example of this in Israel also. The tribe of Dan was allocated land in the area around modern day Tel Aviv on the plains of Sharon. Like all the other tribes they were commanded to go in possess and subdue the land. They chose not to and instead went and possessed land in the far North of Israel. There they instituted a false worship of Baal and the setting up of a false altar which opened a generational gate. Dan's disobedience is what really led Israel off into Idolatry. Tel Dan is the area in which Jeroboam, one of Israel's most wicked kings set up an altar to Baal and made the northern tribes go and worship there instead of in Jerusalem. The area of Dan became the place where Pan Worship developed during Greek and Roman times it became known as the gates of Hell. The same place where Jesus said, "I will build my Church and the gates of Hell shall not prevail against it." Even to this day there is a propensity to have lucky charms and items with the eye of Horus on it in the area of Dan. So, one act of unrepentant disobedience can have generational impact. The same way one act of obedience will have generational impact.

If you look at the life of King David, he opened both good and bad portals. All of them were carried on by his son Solomon. Israel grew under Solomon because David started a process. The temple and pure worship was introduced in Solomon's reign, but David's weakness for a pretty face was accelerated in Solomon. This eventually caused the kingdom to be split and the northern tribes lost.

No one's perfect, and we all have issues handed down, but in Jesus we have been given a way to break off the disobedience of generations past. Through His blood we can turn generational disobedience around, close old portals and open a new one into the heavenly realm. The thing that remains very clear to me is that if these portals are not closed, the issues will raise their head in our lives and ministries. I'm not suggesting going on a witch hunt to find stuff but when the Holy Spirit asks for change or action we need to act quickly in obedience.

This leads me to the main point, when we were in Turkey the question arose, how could a nation that was almost entirely Christian become so barren in Christian life? A nation that at one time was the apostolic power house of the Church, now has only around three thousand known Christians in the midst of a population of seventy seven million.

It soon became obvious to me. Paul and the other Apostles opened huge portals of apostolic authority and within two years the entire region had been impacted. This apostolic foundation was continued for 300 years and growth continued. Antioch and Ephesus became the mission sending centre of the world. The foundation was still Apostolic and the Church was very Hebrew in its thinking. Then in 326AD the church, shifted from apostolic power to the council of men.

The first of the seven general councils of the Church; the council in Nicea, expelled all Jews and divorced the church from Jewish thinking. The second council in Ephesus introduced the worship of Mary. The very seat of Diana worship became the place worship of Mary was introduced. Other councils, seven in total, introduced Icon worship and other abominations over a three hundred and sixty year period, thus the doors opened by the Apostles were closed and doors to the demonic were now wide open. Thus Turkey and the Church were plunged into darkness and within two hundred and fifty years of the first council, the Church shifted from apostolic government to the council of men. The vacuum created by the lack of apostolic government was filled by the highly organized Islamic faith from about 620 AD and the Church dived off into the dark ages as a result. Reformation and recovery has been underway for several centuries now, however there is still a way to go.

The pattern for how the church is supposed to look is in Heaven. When we declare "As it is in heaven so shall it be on earth" we are declaring a vision of foundations, borders, boundaries and gates. In Revelation 21 there is a vision of the New Jerusalem. How it looks in Heaven and what we are declaring on earth.

Revelation 21:10-14
So he took me in spirit to a great, high mountain, and he showed me the holy city, Jerusalem, descending out of Heaven from God. It was filled with the glory of God and sparkled like a precious gem, crystal clear like jasper. Its walls were broad and high, with twelve gates guarded by twelve angels. And the names of the twelve tribes of Israel were written on the gates. There were three gates on each side-east, north, south, and west. The wall of the city had twelve

foundation stones, and on them were written the names of the twelve apostles of the Lamb.

It was filled with the Glory of God; this is what we are looking for, "as it is in heaven so shall it be on earth"

Its foundations are the twelve Apostles. The atmosphere is glory and it is full of gates, in other words the foundation laid by the apostolic is our foundation as well. The Church has been in a period of darkness because it has been operating on the foundation of the council of men and dismissed its true apostolic foundation.

It's time to repent, a time to bring the wrong from the council of men and bring it under the blood of Jesus, into true apostolic authority. What does this apostolic government look like?

Apostolic confronts. - Paul in Acts 19 is a good example of apostolic confrontation of spiritual powers. He took on Artemus (Diana) and won. He closed a portal and opened a new one. Peter opened a portal for the Gentiles at Cornelius house, Philip opened a door into transportation and so on. The whole Church is called to operate from this apostolic foundation of gate opening and the release of the Kingdom of Heaven on earth as it is in Heaven.

The Apostolic releases the power of Heaven. Acts 2 showed us the intention of the Holy Spirit in building his church. There's no sickness suffering or sorrow in Heaven and the apostolic foundation released this on earth. The Church was born in the revelation of heaven's glory and power. The council of men has dulled our understanding of true apostolic.

The Apostolic released women. Contrary to popular belief, the apostolic released women into leadership and the fullness of the power of God. The New Testament reveals that in the second Adam, Jesus, we are restored back into the unity the first Adam had before the fall. Male and female reflect the image of God, each in a unique way, one is not greater than the other. We will know that true apostolic reformation has arrived when we see Adam reflected in this way again as it was in the beginning.

The Apostolic releases us into fellowship and feasting. Our celebration went from the ritual and form of the old Jewish system into the fellowship and celebration of the early Church. With the retreat back into the council of men, the fellowship and feasting reverted back to form.

The Apostolic released a Kingdom on earth. Jesus declared it and the apostles released it. The release of the Kingdom in the early Church was so revolutionary, that within two hundred years the world was a different place. Kings and princes yielded to the King of kings. I hope you get the drift. The council of men took apostolic authority and said only a few men have power, when in actual fact the apostolic foundation allows all believers to move in this power. The only way the Kingdom will be released on earth as it is in Heaven, is to set the Sons and Daughters free, and to open the gates for them. This is the season to walk again on the foundation of the apostles, not to lay new ones but to release the original plan. Push aside all the rubbish the council of men has bought in over the centuries and move forward by stepping back into the perfect plan of laid down by true apostolic government.

The gates in Revelation are the twelve tribes (less Dan but plus Levi.) The Nicene council put the Jews out of the Church but God still has them in the gates of the eternal city.

According to Romans 11 the Gentiles are grafted into the root stock which is Israel. Romans 11:15 says "the acceptance of the Jews is life from the dead."

He says that if branches were broken off to allow Gentiles (wild olives) to be grafted in how much easier is it to graft back in the true branches? We are coming into a season when the church will again recognise her Jewish roots, start thinking Jewish and not Greek and walk in the favour of the God of Abraham.

Jewish thinking sees every aspect of life as spiritual. Greek thinking separates natural and spiritual, therefore if you think Greek there are no consequences for our natural actions. Hebrew thinking however would see everything as having a consequence. There is an end time thinking that is about to be released into the Church again. For nearly one thousand six hundred and fifty years the church has been thinking Greek. There is a call to repent for our acceptance of the Nicene council and its expulsion of the Jews. It's time to see Romans 11:15 fulfilled in our time.

There is a Messianic move happening in Israel it's exciting and it's a signal that we are entering a new season. When the former (Jews) and latter (Gentile church) come together, its life from the dead, its resurrection glory.

The Holy Spirit is calling us to come as one new man in Messiah moving in apostolic foundations and gates of glory. In order to do this we must move from old ways and thinking and allow this reformation to be activated in our lives. This will require repentance from mindsets and attitudes that stop us seeing the heavenly pattern.

Rev 21 says, the city is filled with the glory of God and sparkles like a precious gem, crystal clear like jasper. Its walls were broad and high, with twelve gates guarded by twelve angels.

This is what the Church is about to look like, reformation is at hand, things are about to shift and change. This is Life from the dead.

To follow up then we need to recognize the wrong foundations, borders and gates in the foundation of the Church. The 1514 reformation started the process, but in most cases we haven't addressed the error of some of the seven general councils of the church. One of the most important ones being that we need to repent from the edicts of the Nicean council in divorcing the Church from its Jewish foundation.

NOTES.

NOTES

A KINGDOM
OF
INTIMACY

A KINGDOM OF INTIMACY

The Christian faith is about relationship, it's not about religion or outward displays of Church life that are just forms and religious expressions. Jesus spoke very firmly to the religious of the day, who felt they were doing the right thing in preserving religious tradition but ignoring its core values.

Matt 23:13, "What sorrow awaits you teachers of religious law and you Pharisees? Hypocrites! For you shut the door of the Kingdom of Heaven in people's faces. You won't go in yourselves, and you don't let others enter either.V15 For you cross land and sea to make one convert, and then you turn that person into twice the child of hell V16 you say that it means nothing to swear 'by God's Temple,' but that it is binding to swear 'by the gold in the Temple.V23 you are careful to tithe even the tiniest income but you ignore the more important aspects of the law—justice, mercy, and faith V25 For you are so careful to clean the outside of the cup and the dish, but inside you are filthy—full of greed and self-indulgence."

Jesus didn't mince words; he said it like it is. I am concerned enough about aspects of the current Church model to speak out also. I am concerned because I see a trend in Church life which points to the passages in Matt 23.

I am constantly coming across people from very large and "successful" churches that have all the right words about commitment, giving, and honour. They say they are living a blessed life and they trumpet their life lessons and success, saying that if it wasn't for their Church/Pastor they would not be living this wonderful life they now live. Sounds all very good, but there is never any mention of Jesus or the work of the Holy Spirit. In fact many of these so called Pentecostal Christians haven't even been baptized in water or in the Holy Spirit. On deeper questioning most look at me blank if I start to talk about a deep inner communion with Christ or a Holy Spirit inspired move of signs and wonders. Brothers and Sisters we have a problem. The words of Jesus in Matt 23 are very pertinent to today's situation.

 Jesus asked the question "which is holy? The offering placed on the altar or the altar that made the offering holy?" I ask the same question which is holy the Church, or Jesus who makes the Church holy? An intelligent person will always say "it's Jesus" but the outward actions of our Churches declare another belief.

The outward nature of the Church is very important because without it we will see no souls touched or saved. Without an inward expression it is dead and powerless.

What is an inward expression you ask? Psalm 23 says "He prepares a table for me in the presence of my enemies." It's a table for two in the wilderness; the food is union with Christ. This table is where our hunger for Him is satisfied. So in our obsession with the outward expression of the Church in the world we have lost sight of the table for two. The table for two is where all of the signs, wonders and miracles of Church history come from. It's an intimate table that when you are there no one else knows, so because of this many don't ever accept the invitation of the Lord to come and dine. There is no point in their minds to this table where no one sees them. Jesus responds this way, "For you are so careful to clean the outside of the cup and the dish, but inside you are filthy—full of greed and self-indulgence."

The call to come inward to the table is often ignored because many don't see the value of such fellowship; their aim is to be doing, where as the aim of the table for two is simply "being" in His presence.

The truth is only Christ can fill our empty hearts and satisfy our hunger but because we are mostly outward in our focus it's difficult to see that in His body and His blood lie our total provision.

So how are we to approach this table for two? The answer is simple: we approach the table with hunger. We come with the intention of an intimate meal shared with the King. Any thoughts of what will we get out of this meal diminish its true value. The value of being alone with Him, a place where we can laugh or cry, a place where we can totally bear our soul, confess our love and open our hearts to His light. This sort of intimacy is never found in Church. Church is where what we have found at the table for two becomes public and outward in its expression. With just the outward expression we only have one face of a two sided coin and to the world that's what the Church has become, a faceless coin that once had some value but now is worthless.

"Popular Church services can provide giddy or glitzy God talk that makes us feel religious without providing any real time with God." (Calvin Miller)

The soul is fed with CD's and books promising instant wealth or guaranteed success if we follow the system, whereas our spirit is yearning for an intimate table for two in the wilderness of His love. The soul food that is filling the Church is just junk food in expensive wrappers. The so called obesity crisis in the western world bought on by a constant diet of junk food that might taste good but has no real nutritional value is the same crisis facing the western church. We eat junk we become fat, we die. All the time we gorge ourselves on the junk food there is a table for two with the best of fare set in the wilderness. The food we so long for and desire to fill our hunger is only found in Christ, but the constant sermons and books tell us that in order to be well we must eat their branded junk food and forget the wacky wilderness dwellers who got left behind in the midst of the last century, much the same as the mystics got left behind in the excitement of the reformation in 1514.

The thing about the table for two in the wilderness is that some who attend stay for such a short time, hurriedly swallowing as much as they can in order to fulfill the demands of time, when the table is set in eternity, where constraints of time hold no sway. It's a learnt experience to become a dweller at the table where we take small bites and savor each one gaining the full expression of Christ in each morsel in whom we partake. The Church fathers spoke of Otium Sanctum which is a relaxed contemplation of the indwelling Christ. A pace impossible to find in a world filled with busy works orientated religion.

Much of what has become known as worship is just a performance of good music in a Church setting with little or no thought of leading the worshiper into a divine encounter at a table for two in the wilderness. True worship creates intimacy and intimacy leads to the table set for two. Performance based worship, at best, brings an awareness of our hunger but will always fail to satisfy our spirits desire for intimacy with the King. True worship is only achieved in the company of the King and His Company is best received at the table for two in the wilderness.

Our quest for wealth and possessions can hinder our focus. It's not wrong to have wealth, it's just wrong for the wealth and possessions to control our way to the table. When our heart would rather own things than be owned by Christ we have entered into the Western Church model that says' "True spiritual abundance is measured by the wealth you exhibit and the possessions you have," we loose our connection with reality. Are men drawn to Christ by our expression of wealth and if so, what sort of Christ are we drawing them to? The finest Christians I have ever met live without much in the way of material possessions in very poor nations. Is their Jesus whom they meet with at a table in the wilderness the same one the Western Church longs for? Again I want to point out that it's not wrong to have possessions, it's just wrong for the possessions to block our way to the King's table. Jesus said, "If any man comes after me he must deny himself and take up His cross daily," Luke 9:23. There is a laying down in order to come into the fellowship around the table.

Hebrews11:6 says, "without faith it is impossible to please God" This is the great truth of the gospel often overlooked, because in our western worldview Church we have equated Church commitment with a commitment to Christ, in doing this we have lost sight of the table set for two in the wilderness. True life is found in our faith led walk into the inward place, a place we can enter only by faith. So come step into this inward mystical journey that leads you to true fellowship with God. Step into it by faith and eat of its fare with abandonment.

Why a table for two? It is because in this union with Christ we become released into the fullness of His desires for us. Eastern religion demands that you come on an inward journey in order to empty yourself of sound and desires; however the invitation to the table for two is an inner conversation with the King filled with delight, conversations and feasting.

This chapter is an invitation to abandonment, a call to discover that true life is expressed in Inward and outward expressions of this abandonment. This is a rescue call from the Holy Spirit to a Church lost in form and religion, a call to return to the flow of the Holy Spirit.

There is a place before God known only between you and God. Everyone sees and knows the things revealed but the secret things, the things gained in the place of intimacy, belong to God.

Are there yet things that man doesn't know? Yes of course! In Israel at En Gedi, the place where David hid form King Saul, we saw the mountain Ibex a lovely little mountain deer. When God was questioning Job one of his questions related to the Ibex He asked in Job 39:1, "Do you know when the mountain Ibex gives birth? Or can you mark where the hinds do calve?"

The amazing thing is; that to this day no one has ever observed the Ibex giving birth, it's one of the mysteries of life. The fact that you see little Ibex running everywhere, plus the fact that they still exist as a species tells us that although this mystery has not been observed, it is happening.

In a place of intimacy the Ibex obeys the voice of God generation after generation and the result is new life that seemingly appears from nowhere.

We are called to that place of intimacy before the Lord as well. Before anything else we are called to walk in this place known only to God and shared with His Sons and Daughters. In that place before the face of God there are transactions that occur and life that is imparted that cannot be found in any teaching or program or even human relationship. The true latter rain of His Sprit is found in the face of God.

Proverbs 16:15, In the light of the king's face is life, and his favor is like a cloud of the latter rain.

Jesus is our example in seeking the face of the Father. He did nothing without coming before the Father and looking into His face. There are plenty of activities around to take our focus off the main thing, but when God invades our lives things change. So in these transactions or times before His face, the secret things of our heart are exposed to the all knowing power of the living God. His voice demands a response and there is a shout of glory that rises up in our spirit.

Psalm 29:9, "The voice of the Lord makes the deer (Ibex) to calve and strips the forest bare; and in His temple everything shouts glory".

1 Cor 2:9, "No eye has seen, no ear has heard, and no mind has imagined what God has prepared for those who love him".

Eyes, Ears and our minds can't contain all that is God. In the secret place before Him, in that place of intimacy, that which we can't perceive in our natural senses can be perceived in the spirit. In the same way as the Ibex just knows where to go to have her young, so we, as we spend time in intimacy with God, will have a knowing of His ways come upon us. Some call it instinct, some call it intuition but really it's an impartation from the creator of the universe. It cannot be comprehended in the natural.

In the natural, our senses; taste, touch, see, hear, and smell, cannot comprehend God and his fullness. Yet in the Spirit we are given eyes to see the invisible, ears to hear the inaudible, minds that conceive the inconceivable.

Smith Wigglesworth in one of his fiery sermons in Wellington, New Zealand in 1922, shouted out. "Come out of your soul and into the spirit."

The soul is ever learning and always wanting to be fed but until we put the soul in it's place and surrender our spirit in intimate connection with the Lord our journey remains dry. We are called to dwell in the secret place of the most high. To gaze upon His beauty; to nestle into his heart; for our heart's home is in the midst of His heart. The unseen power of Wigglesworth's ministry was his intimate connection to the Lord.

1 Cor 2:10, "But we know these things because God has revealed them to us by his Spirit and his Spirit searches out everything and shows us even God's deep secrets".

It is only in moving out of our soul and into the Spirit that we enter into the fullness of intimacy. We are touched even in the very deep regions of the heart. God's vastness viewed through natural eyes overwhelms us in our soul. This stimulates a response from our spirit. In this intimacy we begin to "SEE" in the realms of the spirit, and like the Ibex, we begin to do things that appear secret to this realm. It becomes a natural outworking of who we are and what we are called to be.

For instance after years of Christian teaching that caused my eyes to be closed in the Spirit instead of open, I met Kathie Walters, an amazing ministry from the USA and I started to move into the realms of seeing in the Spirit. I entered places of intimacy with the Lord because my mindset was challenged by Kathie's ministry and I was able to "SEE" clearly the things I was always meant to see. I stepped out of the soul realm of taste not, touch not, handle not, which most of the Church has bought into and stepped into the spiritual realm. In this realm I saw Heaven and angels and chariots, the entire realm of the Spirit which is where we are called to dwell and rule from. Not in the soulish realms of programs and events that stir the soul but neglect the Spirit.

Like the Ibex, some things remain between me and the Lord but also like the Ibex, the fruit of this intimacy is there for all to see. My Angelic encounters and encounters in Heaven and in unseen places have all borne, or have the potential, to bear fruit in the natural or seen realm.

My encounters in the Spirit that saw me carried to Israel have all borne fruit and the nations I have been carried to in the spirit have all opened to me for ministry. Some have said to me "what is the purpose of all these encounters? My answer is clear; for me my encounters are like a forerunning intercession that opens the way for me to release something of Heaven into the places I'm called to go. Every where I have been carried in the Spirit I am confident I will go in the natural.

In 2006 I had some interesting encounters with angels and chariots that took me over much of New Zealand and gave me a prophetic understanding of the call over the nation and also the call over regions within the nation. Many of the things I spoke out at that time have come to pass, many things have yet to come to pass but I am confident that they will.

All this happened, because I allowed my mindsets to be changed so that I saw with eyes that see the invisible, ears that hear the inaudible, and a mind that conceives the inconceivable.

We all have the Ability; every believer has this ability and is meant to be walking in it. Sadly the greatest opponents are other Christians with religious spirits who hate the idea of the body of Christ seeing in the spirit. The devil knows that if the church sees, his tricks will be revealed and will be exposed, so of course the religious spirit is working overtime to put this revolution down.

But like Wigglesworth I continue to say, "Come out of your soul and into the spirit."

Come out of the council of men and into apostolic authority. This is the resurrection authority that tore down the wall between the realm of the Spirit and the natural realm. Intimacy and seeing in the Spirit releases resurrection life and power.

In Portugal, I spoke to a youth service and the Lord asked me to proclaim life; mainly because Portugal has been in the hold of a strong death spirit. What I was seeing in the Spirit as I proclaimed life or 'vida', was a gate opening that had been closed for generations. I saw angels coming into the land that had been prevented for generations. I literally saw life flooding in. Did the enemy like this? No of course not, the next day the train I was traveling on hit a woman on the tracks and parts of her body were cast against my window and we screeched to a halt. It was a terrible experience but I realised that death was not happy with what I had achieved by being in the Spirit.

I believe we need to keep pressing into the realms of the Spirit, to come to the place where every thing we do is generated in the Spirit and out of Heaven. Our role is to break down mindsets that prevent the Sons and Daughters of the most high from entering their full inheritance, which is the spiritual realm.

In order to truly see the move of God that will bring in the billions that need to be saved in a very short space of time, we are going to have to move into new levels of coming into intimacy and union with Christ, and out of this intimacy a seeing and hearing in the Spirit. It's time to stop playing games and putting our toes in the water to test the temperature; instead, we need to jump headlong into the realm of the spirit. Union and intimacy is the true hallmark of Apostolic Messianic Prophetic Christianity.

This is a call for reformation out of a faith based on principles into a faith based on a kingdom reality. Like the Ibex, many may not get to see the birth of this new move but all will see the fruit of this reformation and birth, because God had ordained that the Ibex would breed after her kind and life would flourish. He has also ordained that his sons and Daughters would bring forth resurrection life and multiply by entering into the realm of the Spirit where the atmosphere is life and glory. Come and join me in this intimacy and in this reformation. Intimacy in a marriage union usually results in the birth of children. So too, intimacy with the bridegroom on by the bride of Christ brings forth new fruit.

A soul bound by religious duty can only be obedient to the boundaries the religion provides, and this striving to please proves tiresome. A soul in total union with Christ is a soul full of joy because He (Jesus), has completed the work. Therefore obedience to Christ is the highest form of worship, and rest in our soul is its fruit.

So how do we come into this rest of soul, this union with Christ? Well it's not by striving to attain or working to please, for He has achieved a finished work for us. These words still echo from the cross, "It is finished." Yet religion always strives to perfect the perfect.

The Holy Spirit leads us into fellowship with Jesus and brings us to the Father to gaze on His beauty. It is here that perfection has its way. It is in this gaze that we are transformed from slaves to saints. Nothing else can bring us to this point only our yielding to the invitations of the wonderful Holy Spirit.

We become what we gaze upon! Therefore it stands to reason that if we gaze upon the beauty of the Father we will ultimately become one who is truly found in His image. If we observe the words of the Holy Spirit and allow Him to lead us into the heart of Jesus our hearts are transformed into the nature of a Son and not that of a slave.

When Jesus was on earth as a man, He learnt obedience to the Father and through this obedience the glory increased in his earthly form and the weight of heaven manifested on earth as it is in heaven. He has shown us the gateway to this weighty glory; it is to gaze, to rest and to obey.

The thing that dismisses this weighty glory more than anything else is a striving to be perfect. The Holy Spirit invites us to step into Jesus because He has mastered, and is in Himself, perfection. In Jesus we have access to the throne room of His majesty not by our own work but by virtue of His. Not by our own lineage or position, but by His, in stepping into Him we take on the authority of Sonship.

The matter of Sonship needs to be grasped by us in order for us to walk freely in and out of His glory. We never come boasting but we can come confident of His welcome because the words of the cross, "It is finished" are engraved on us. In order to come into this place of gazing all we have to do is enter through Jesus. His invitation is there for all to come boldly. But don't come through religion and don't come without first coming into Christ, but what ever you do, please come.

ABOUT THE AUTHOR

Saved in 1977 as a result of a face to face encounter with Jesus, Ian Johnson has always sought to live in a life of encounter and intimacy with the Lord. With a heart for history, Ian has discovered that in every century the Church has demonstrated the supernatural. He has made it his mission to communicate the mystical and supernatural realm of the Kingdom of God to this current generation.

Ian has been in ministry for over twenty five years having pioneered and led Churches in the South Auckland area of New Zealand.

Ian and Joye Johnson travel as itinerant ministers speaking in Churches and conferences in NZ, Australia and the nations. Currently Ian is on the leadership team at Horizon Church in Auckland, New Zealand.

His Amazing Glory Ministries

Ian & Joye Johnson travel the nation & the nations opening up prophetic and supernatural understanding in the body of Christ. They are based at Horizon Church in Auckland New Zealand where they are part of the governmental leadership team. Ian speaks at Church and conferences as a sought after prophetic ministry.

To book Ian Johnson for Church or Conference speaking or supernatural ministry training engagements contact the ministry by e-mail ianjohn@xtra.co.nz

View our Web-site www.hisamazinggloryministries.org

His Amazing Glory Facebook page.

OTHER TITLES BY IAN JOHNSON

Glory to Glory
A Journey of Intimacy & Worship

Into the heart of Jesus
A 21 day journey into an Intimate walk

Anzac's Israel & God
The ANZAC legacy & modern Israel

Man on a Mission
The supernatural ministry of Francis Xavier.
Also available as an E-book on Amazon Kindle under the title THE MIRACLES OF FRANCIS XAVIER

Gems from Heaven
A collection of quotes from the ministry of Ian Johnson

All titles Available From
**His Amazing Glory Ministries
4 Ewing Road RD4 Tuakau
2694, New Zealand.**

**Ph (09)2368126
E-mail ianjohn@xtra.co.nz**

All titles also available at www.amazon.com as Paperbacks or as an E-book.

Made in the USA
Middletown, DE
07 November 2016